WORLDS APART

WORLDS APART

William MacDonald

GOSPEL FOLIO PRESS
P. O. Box 2041, Grand Rapids MI 49501-2041
Available in the UK from
JOHN RITCHIE LTD., Kilmarnock, Scotland

Cover design by J. B. Nicholson, Jr.

Published by Gospel Folio Press
P. O. Box 2041, Grand Rapids, MI 49501-2041

ISBN 1-882701-05-4

Printed in the United States of America

CONTENTS

PREFACE

It greatly simplifies matters once we realize that basically there are only two kingdoms. There is the kingdom which the Bible calls "the world," and there is the kingdom of God, also called the kingdom of our Lord and Saviour Jesus Christ. They are worlds apart.

Dec. 1993

Dear Marili

The paragraph above is true and the decision is ours to make — our choice determines our eternal destiny and whether we have peace or conflict in our hearts during our earthly life[7] — Which is it for you, dear grand daughter?

1

THE WORLD: A KINGDOM OF DARKNESS

When we speak of the world in this sense, we do not mean planet earth, which God has given us as a temporary dwelling place. Nor do we mean the world of nature, which God has given to us to enjoy. And we certainly don't mean the world of mankind, which God expects us to love as He does (Jn. 3:16). What then do we mean?

The world is the civilization which man has built up in order to fulfill his desires without God. It is not only independent of God, but opposed to Him. The world system is founded on wrong principles and promotes false values. It is largely self-centered. Wealth, power, and sex are central in its culture. "All civilization without God, from the beginning, has been stamped with His curse; and what men call improvement, and inventions, and progress, without God, seems simply to be the erection of a Babel tower, essentially idolatrous, and the center of self-glory."[1]

The whole society is inspired and energized by Satan. Just as holy angels are guardians of God's people, so demon powers are active in the affairs of the evil empire.

An Empty Show

Actually the world is empty. It is a facade. It is a sick joke. All it offers cannot satisfy the human heart. A whole book of the Bible—Ecclesiastes—is dedicated to exposing the vanity of the world of life under the sun. Malcolm Muggeridge realized this; he wrote: "Human life, I have come to feel, in all its public or collective manifestations is only theater, and mostly cheap melodrama at that."[2]

Someone else said, "The world's way is make-believe; the kingdom is eternal reality." People of the world are trying to get more out of it than there is in it.

And yet it is very attractive to people. It presents itself as the *summum bonum,* the greatest good. People are dazzled by its psychedelic lights, its contemporary music, its sensuous clothes. Everyone in Marlboro country is good looking, owns a horse, and leans against the front fender of a convertible, charming or being charmed by a beauty queen. It's a never, never land—an artificial society. It is glitz and glitter without worthwhile substance.

What is Worldly?

Worldliness is the love of passing things. It is anything that pulls a believer away from the Lord. A worldly person is one whose plans all end at the grave. Jowett said it well: "Worldliness is a spirit, a temper. It is not so much an act as an attitude. It is a pose, a posture . . . Worldliness is human activity with God left out. Worldliness is life without heavenly callings, life without ideals, life without heights. Worldliness recognizes nothing of the high calling of God in Christ Jesus. It has no hill country. It is horizontal life. Worldliness has nothing of the vertical in it. It has ambition; it has no aspirations. Its motto is success, not holiness. It is always saying 'Onward,' never 'Upward.' A worldly man or woman is a man or woman who never says, 'I will lift up mine eyes unto the hills.'"[3]

In some circles, the definition of worldliness has been largely confined to drinking, smoking, gambling, dancing, card playing, movies, and similar activities. It is wider than that. Dr. Dale wrote, "To be worldly is to permit the higher law to which we owe allegiance, the glories and terrors of that invisible universe which is revealed to faith, our transcendent relations to the Father of spirits through Christ Jesus our Lord, to be overborne by inferior interests."

"My brother, if you go back and live a worldly life, you have to go back through the grave to it, because the grave lies between the body of Christ, of which you are a part, and the world that cast Him out. The world cast Him out, and we were buried in Christ by the world that hates the church."[4]

There is a limit to the divine patience with one who tries to get the best of both worlds.

2

THE KINGDOM THAT MATTERS

In sharp contrast to all this is the kingdom of our Lord and Saviour Jesus Christ. In this realm, the spiritual is emphasized over the soulish; the eternal is valued over the temporal. Pleasure is not despised, but it is sought in its purest form and in its only true source.

> *I thirst, but not as once I did,*
> *The vain delights of earth to share;*
> *Thy wounds, Emmanuel, all forbid*
> *That I should seek my pleasure there.*
>
> *It was the sight of Thy dear cross*
> *That weaned my heart from earthly things,*
> *And taught me to esteem as dross*
> *The mirth of fools and pomp of kings.*
> —William Cowper

In Christ's kingdom, wealth is not something to be coveted; spiritual prosperity is what really counts. The kingdom of heaven is concerned with righteousness, peace, and joy. Christ, not self, is central. Everything is valued only as it appears in His sight. Whereas men of the world love money and lightly esteem God, subjects of Christ's kingdom lightly esteem money and love God.

3

THE EVIL EMPEROR OF THE WORLD

Since there are only two kingdoms, this means, of necessity, that there are only two rulers: Satan and Christ. The devil is the world's monarch. He is called the ruler of this world (Jn. 12:31; 14:30; 16:11), the god of this age (2 Cor. 4:4), and the prince of the power of the air, the spirit who now works in the sons of disobedience (Eph. 2:2b). The apostle John reminds us flatly that "the whole world lies under the sway of the wicked one" (1 Jn. 5:19). People are held captive by him, and must be awakened from their sleep of death. While the devil is very powerful, he is not omnipotent, and he is still under the dominion of Christ.

The devil is the worst enemy of Christ and therefore of His followers. The other two foes are the world and the flesh. Just as the devil is opposed to Christ, so the world is opposed to the Father and the flesh to the Spirit. This trinity of evil has been described as follows: The devil is the enemy against us; the world is the foe around us; and the flesh is the traitor within us.

His Bag of Tricks

We are not unaware of the devil's devices. Think of the methods he employs:

Deceit. He is the father of lies, and has been lying from the beginning (Jn. 8:44). He poses as an angel of light and sends out his messengers disguised as ministers of righteousness (2 Cor. 11:14-15). He misquotes the Word of God (Gen. 3:1). He performs miracles and lying wonders (2 Thess. 2:9). He seeks to sow doubts and denials, and to divert God's people from sincere and pure devotion to Christ (2 Cor. 11:3). He tempts people to lie (Acts 5:3).

Slander. He is the accuser of the brethren night and day (Rev. 12:10).

Imitation. He has a counterfeit for everything that is of God. He empowered the Egyptian magicians to imitate the miracles of Moses (2 Tim. 3:8). The tares in the kingdom (sons of the wicked one) imitate the wheat (sons of the kingdom) (Mt. 13:38). As J. Oswald Sanders says, "Not without reason did Augustine term him *Simius Dei,* the ape of God. He has his own "trinity": the devil, the beast, and the false prophet; his own church: the synagogue of Satan (Rev. 2:9); his own ministers: ministers of Satan (2 Cor. 11:15); his own gospel: another gospel (Gal. 1:6); his own theology: doctrines of devils (1 Tim. 4:1); his own sacrifices: sacrifices offered to demons (1 Cor. 10:20); his own table and cup (1 Cor. 10:21-22)."[5]

Discouragement. It is a satanic ploy to take advantage of Christians by causing them to be "swallowed up with too much sorrow," that is, to be discouraged (2 Cor. 2:7-11). Also he can oppress the believer with gloom and despair.

Persecution. He goes about as a roaring lion to terrify and destroy (1 Pet. 5:8; Rev. 2:10). In fact, the invariable purpose of this thief is to kill and steal and destroy (Jn. 10:10).

Incomplete Commitment. Just as he sought to dissuade Jesus from going to the cross (Mk. 8:31-33), so he seeks to dissuade Christians from bearing the cross.

Pride. He knows by personal experience that pride goes before destruction (1 Tim. 3:6). So he uses this device on others.

Moral Failure. He tempts people because of their lack of self-control (1 Cor. 7:5).

False Doctrine. At the dawn of human civilization, he tempted Eve to believe that she could become like God (Gen. 3:5).

Bodily Affliction. Paul's thorn in the flesh was a messenger of Satan to buffet him (2 Cor. 12:7). The devil sifts God's people by difficult circumstances (Lk. 22:31). All sickness, suffering, and tragedy are from him, but in the life of the believer God can overrule them for His glory, for the Christian's good, and for the blessing of others.

Hindering of the gospel. He snatches away the seed from shallow listeners (Mt. 13:19). Also he blinds the minds of unbelievers lest they should see the truth and be saved (2 Cor. 4:4).

Procrastination. He moves people to delay, to put off the time of action and decision, especially with regard to the gospel.

17

4
KING JESUS!

The Lord Jesus, of course, is the ruler of the other kingdom. He is no less than the Creator and Upholder of the universe. He has what no other king has—all knowledge, all power, and all presence, that is, He is everywhere. Perfect God and perfect Man, He is also the perfect Saviour from sin. He combines in His Person every excellence, every beauty, virtue, and grace.

He is infinite, unique, and incomparable. At the present time, He reigns from His throne in heaven over all who acknowledge Him as their supreme Monarch. Soon He will return to earth as King of kings and Lord of lords, and reign over the earth with Jerusalem as His capital.

5

THE WORLD'S CITIZENS

All unconverted people belong to the world. They are found in every level of society—from the cream to the dregs. Many are outwardly moral, decent folks, the kind that make good neighbors. Others, of course, are immoral, depraved, and lawless. One thing they have in common is their unwillingness to acknowledge the Lord Jesus Christ as their Lord and Saviour.

They walk "according to the course of this world, according to the prince of the power of the air, the spirit who now works in the sons of disobedience" (Eph. 2:2). The god of this age has blinded their minds "lest the light of the gospel of the glory of Christ . . . should shine on them" (2 Cor. 4:4). Through fear of death, they are subject to lifelong bondage (Heb. 2:15).

They are at home in the world, they love the world, and the world loves them (Jn. 15:19). They are enemies of God, held in the grip of the devil. David described them as "men of the world who have their portion in this life" (Ps. 17:14).

6

CITIZENS OF THE HOLY KINGDOM

Christians are Aliens

Believers, on the other hand, are strangers and pilgrims on the earth (1 Pet. 2:11). For them the world is a poor home, but a good school. They are traveling through the world to their own country, committed to take none of the world's character upon themselves. As Jesus reminded His disciples, they are in the world but not of it (Jn. 17:11, 14, 16). As He is, so are they in the world (1 Jn. 4:17). Paul likens them to ambassadors, sent from heaven to represent the Lord in this world (2 Cor. 5:20).

In this connection, Vance Havner commented, "When Jacob brought all his family to Egypt at the invitation of Joseph, they settled in Egypt in 'the country of Goshen.' Today God's people, the Church, of the kingdom of heaven, live in Egypt, as it were—in this world but not of it. They are a spiritual colony of heaven. Not citizens of earth going to heaven, but citizens of heaven making their way through this world, pilgrims and strangers, exiles and aliens, a holy nation within the nation, the family of God."[6]

J. G. Deck captured the true status of believers when he wrote:

> Called from above, and heavenly men by birth ,
> (Who once were but the citizens of earth),
> As pilgrims here, we seek a heavenly home,
> Our portion in the ages yet to come.

23

> *We are but strangers here, we do not crave*
> *A home on earth, which gave Thee but a grave:*
> *Thy cross has severed ties which bound us here,*
> *Thyself our treasure in a brighter sphere.*

As Philip Hacking said, "We, like Abraham, are called to go out of the world because we're different, and yet to go back into the world because we're salt and light."[7]

Christians do not love the world or the things that are of the world, but seek to do the will of God, knowing that in doing so they will abide forever (1 Jn. 2:15-17). In a very real sense, they are non-conformists, refusing to be poured into the world's mold (Rom. 12:2). "Society demands conformity. If you fall beneath its standards, it will punish you; if you rise above its standards, it will persecute you. It demands a dull, gray, average conformity. But the Christian is a departure upward. He gets out of step, for 'he hears a distant Drummer.' He is no longer an echo; he is a voice. He is not a thing, he is a person. The herd dominance is broken."[8]

The Christian life is a life of intense conflict. As Ronald Dunn said, "It is not a spectator sport viewed from a safe distance. We are in the thick of it, personally involved in the conflict, whether we know it or not."[9] It is not a matter of co-existence or of detente, but it is a positive adversary relationship that the Christian has to Satan's kingdom. He testifies against it that its deeds are evil (Jn. 7:7), and also proclaims the message of reconciliation, namely, that sinful man can be reconciled to God through the work of the Saviour on the cross of Calvary. There God, the Father, "made Him who knew no sin to be sin for us, that we might become the righteousness of God in Him" (2 Cor. 5:21). So while believers are to be insulated from the world, they are not to be isolated. Scriptural separation does not require a monastic life. As someone has said, "The Christian must live in the world, but he must not let the world live in him."

Isaac Watts' hymn reminds us that "this vile world [is not] a friend of grace to help [us] on to God." On the contrary, it is unrelenting in its hostility to us, and determined to wipe out every divine principle for which we stand. It seeks to supplant creationism with evolution. It denies the sacredness of human life by abortion. It achieves the breakdown of the family unit by divorce for any reason. The purity of the marriage relationship is denied by pre-marital sex. Homosexuality and lesbianism are looked on as acceptable alternative lifestyles. God's chain of command in the home and in the church is ridiculed by militant feminism. Church and state are so separated as to ban the mention of God and Christ from public life entirely. Obscenity, pornography, nakedness, filth, and violence are treated with amiable tolerance. And so, drugged and insensate, the world defies every law of God and hurtles on to its fiery doom.

The Rite of Passage

There is a rite of passage from the world to Christ's kingdom. It is known as the new birth. When a person repents of his sins and receives Jesus Christ as Lord and Saviour, he no longer belongs to the world. He has changed his ancestry, his citizenship, and his master. He pictures this transition in water baptism. As he goes under the water, he is saying, in effect, "When Christ died, I died. Since Christ died to sin and the world, I have died to both." As he comes up out of the water, he is expressing his determination to walk in newness of life—as one whose allegiance is henceforth to the true King.

Persecuted for Righteousness' Sake

Christians should not be shocked when they experience the hatred of the world (1 Jn. 3:13). The New Testament is replete with warnings that they should expect it (e.g., Jn. 15:18-19). The Saviour never promised that the believer's life would be free from scorn, ridicule, and even persecution. To the contrary, He assured His own that they would have tribulation (Jn. 16:33). It is a spurious gospel that offers the world's approving smile and a trouble-free existence.

The world hates Christ, so naturally it will hate His followers (Jn. 15:18). The disciple cannot expect better treatment than his Master had on earth (Jn. 15:20). As Spurgeon said, "The world found a cross for the Master, and cannot be expected to award crowns to His disciples."

> *And though here on earth rejected,*
> *'Tis but fellowship with Thee;*
> *What besides could be expected,*
> *Than like Thee, our Lord, to be?*
> *Thou art worthy!*
> *Thou from earth hast set us free.*
> —S. P. Tregelles

Christian-Bashing

The world loves its own (Jn. 15:19)—those who toe the party line. But it has nothing but contempt for non-conforming believers.

Unwillingness to let the world around us squeeze us into its own mold explains why there is so much anti-Christian bigotry in TV and the movies, why there is such a pronounced anti-Christian bias on the radio and in the press. Patrick J. Buchanan observed recently, "We live in an age where the ridicule of blacks is forbidden, where anti-Semitism is punishable by political death, but where Christian-bashing is a popular indoor sport; and films mocking Jesus Christ are considered avant-garde."[10]

David Hesselgrave adds: "Despite the comfortable circumstances in which the majority [of Christians] find themselves, the sobering fact is that the twentieth century has been characterized by a terrible outcropping of opposition to the cause and people of Christ. Moreover, there are few signs of abatement on the horizon. Rather, there are many signs of an increased opposition directed especially to those involved in the spread of the Christian faith."[11]

People of the world who may disagree on many matters can unite in their hostility to Christ. Pharisees and Sadducees, Jews and Gentiles, Pilate and Herod find common ground in their hatred of New Testament Christianity.

Like many others, Lenin could not tolerate Christians who had a death-defying commitment to their Lord and to their faith. He saw them as a serious threat to his political aspirations. On the other hand, he had nothing but contempt for nominal, half-hearted Christians, because he knew that he could easily control them. He was right. Allegiance to the King of kings enables a believer to stand up against the power of an alien regime.

"The more the church looks like the world, talks like the world or operates like the world, the more the world disdains it, for the world can beat the church at everything—except this: living out the life of Christ. That and that alone is our distinctiveness, and in that and that alone is our power."[12]

Often when a person is first saved, he is so enthusiastic, so bubbling with the joy of the Lord, that he expects his unbelieving relatives and friends to trust Christ the first time they hear the gospel. Instead he runs into a hornet's nest of opposition (Mt. 10:34-36). His family accuses him of a holier-than-thou attitude. They were quite comfortable with him when he was a dope head, a drunk, a sex fiend. But now they can't cope with the change that has come into his life. His friends condemn him because he no longer joins them in their wild partying (1 Pet. 4:4). Overnight he has become a weirdo.

The Battle Lines

If the world loves a professing believer, that proves that he has never been genuinely converted (Jn. 15:19). If a person claims to be a Christian and yet loves the world, that proves that the love of the Father is not in him (1 Jn. 2:15b). James states it bluntly: "Adulterers and adulteresses! Do you not know that friendship with the world is enmity with God? Whoever therefore wants to be a friend of the world makes himself an enemy of God" (4:4). The battle lines are clearly drawn.

It is a sad day for a Christian when he is popular with the world. It means that he has so adulterated his message that the offense of the cross is gone. Or it means that his life is no different from the lives of those around him; it does not condemn them. He has drifted with the tide instead of swimming against it. Like a chameleon, he has accommodated himself to his environment. In doing so, he has come under the Saviour's stern denunciation, "Woe to you when all men speak well of you, for so did their fathers to the false prophets" (Lk. 6:26).

God's people need not be intimidated by the world's harmless frown. We follow the One who has overcome the world (Jn. 16:33) and we share in His victory. Greater is He who is in us than he who is in the world (1 Jn. 4:4). That is our guarantee of power. Faith enables us to see the emptiness of the world. It is a passing shadow, has nothing of enduring substance. It cannot give lasting satisfaction, but offers only pleasures of sin for a season.

Actually we should rejoice when we experience the hatred and rejection of the world: when that college professor sneers at our faith; when the people with whom we work write us off as obscurantists; when our own family ridicules us as being out of touch with reality. Most of us will never be arrested or beaten for our faith, or pelted with stones, or burned at the stake. It is a small thing to be verbally abused. Like the early disciples, we should rejoice that we are "counted worthy to suffer shame for His Name" (Acts 5:41).

J. G. Deck had it right when he penned these lines:

> *Master, we would no longer be*
> *At home in that which hated Thee,*
> *But patient in Thy footsteps go,*
> *Thy sorrow as Thy joy to know;*
> *We would—and O confirm the power—*
> *With meekness meet the darkest hour,*
> *By shame, contempt however tried,*
> *For Thou wast scorned and crucified.*

Who is the Idiot?

The subjects of the kingdom of God are an enigma to the people of the world (1 Jn. 3:1b). As Peter says, "They think it strange that you do not run with them in the same flood of dissipation, speaking evil of you" (1 Pet. 4:4). Our aims and attitudes are foreign to them. It could not be otherwise, because we are not of the world, even as Christ was not of the world.

Dostoyevsky paints this picture with exquisite skill in his book, *The Idiot.* The aristocratic society of his day was obsessed with prestige, power, sex, and possessions. Truth was of little concern to them. They constantly engaged in bitter sparring with one another, or in frivolous chitchat. There was endless gossip, but little true nobility of character.

In the midst of all this, Prince Myshkin stood out with glaring eccentricity. He cared nothing for status, wealth, domination, or sexual conquest. What made him conspicuous was that he was a truly beautiful soul.[13]

But this Christ-figure was so unworldly that his contemporaries could not understand him. In their mental confusion, they harbored a love-hate relationship toward him. They could not help but admire the simplicity of his character, but they resented him because his nobility put them in a bad light. To put it bluntly, he was a misfit in society. His failure to conform and his unconventional behavior led to only one conclusion—he was an idiot.

The question then as well as the question now is, "Who is the idiot?"

"The contrast between God's kingdom and man's is stark. The first exercises power by love, the second by law. One leads by serving, the other by driving. God's is concerned with spiritual values—righteousness, peace, and joy; man's with worldly considerations—self-promotion, greed, and political patronage."[14]

7

WHAT THE WORLD OFFERS

The world actually doesn't have much to offer its citizens. It can all be summarized in the words, "the lust of the flesh, the lusts of the eyes, and the pride of life" (1 Jn. 2:16). Here the word lust means appetite. It may refer to sexual desires, but it is wider than that.

The lust of the eyes refers to man's insatiable desire to see ever more persons, places, and things. It loves to feed on whatever stirs up the animal inside, and cares not if it is dishonoring to Christ. The world's movies, television, magazines all appeal to the lust of the eyes. They offer enjoyment of what the flesh desires.

The lust of the flesh covers his craving to fulfill all the appetites of his body. Many of these appetites are not wrong in themselves, but they become wrong when they become the center of life, when they are indulged in excess, and when they are used contrary to the Word of God.

The pride of life is the worldling's preoccupation with his person, possessions, pleasures—when he glories in things that soon must pass away. He lives for the body which in a few short years will be eaten by worms. He lives for money which will buy him everything but heaven. He lives for pleasure which cannot provide lasting satisfaction. The pride of life includes the desire for status and prestige, for fame and publicity, for wealth, and for honors.

In a word, the lust of the eyes, the lust of the flesh, and the pride of life add up to self-indulgence.

Oh, what is all the world can give—
I'm called to share in God's own joy;
Dead to the world, in Thee I live,
In Thee I've bliss without alloy;
Well may I earthly joys resign;
All things are mine; and I am Thine.
                    —Author unknown

8

ALL THIS AND HEAVEN TOO

What the Lord offers is, by contrast, out of this world. Let us think of some of the possessions of those who belong to Christ's kingdom. And remember—this is only a sample package.

They know *love* in a newer, truer way than ever before. They experience the love of God, their Father, and the love of all the redeemed (1 Jn. 3:1). This is in sharp contrast to the lust that the world offers.

Joy is another benefit that accompanies salvation (Rom. 14:17). It is the inexpressible ecstasy that springs from relationship to the Lord. His precious promises are a constant source of joy. Unlike the world's happiness, it does not depend on favorable circumstances.

The Saviour brings *peace* with God because Christ has effectively dealt with the cause of hostility, namely, sin. And He offers peace of heart and conscience because the work of redemption is finished, and we are objects of the Father's ceaseless care. He said, "Peace I leave with you, My peace I give to you; not as the world gives do I give to you. Let not your heart be troubled, neither let it be afraid" (Jn. 14:27).

The Christian's *hope* is distinctive because it has no element of doubt or uncertainty in it. The prospect of a glorified body in a heavenly home is certain because it is based on the promise of God.

Of all the believer's material possessions on earth, the most precious is *the Bible*—the inspired, inerrant Word of God. It contains all that is necessary for life and godliness.

Included in the gift of salvation is the unspeakable privilege of *prayer*, of having audience with the Sovereign of the universe at any time of the day or night. The child of God knows that every prayer is answered according to infinite wisdom, love, and power.

Not least among our blessings is *the forgiveness of sins*. Who can measure the relief of knowing that a person's sins have been forgiven and forgotten, that he will never have to pay their penalty because the blood of Christ, shed on Calvary, has provided full satisfaction!

And the child of God is guaranteed *freedom from the dominion of sin*. Although he may commit isolated acts of sin, it is no longer the ruling power in his life. Its reign has been broken.

We must not forget to mention *deliverance from hell*. The Christian will never experience the eternal horrors of the lake of fire because the Lord Jesus endured them as his Substitute on the Cross.

Salvation brings us into a *worldwide family*, the fellowship of the redeemed. This has nothing to do with denominations or organizations. It is the blood-bought family of God. The ties that bind in this spiritual fellowship are closer than mere human relationships.

The *guidance* of God is still another perk for all who belong to Christ. When we obey His leading, it guarantees a life of fulfillment. At last, we have something to live for and Someone to die for.

We can add *help when needed* to the list of our priceless possessions. The Holy Spirit, our Paraclete, comes alongside to assist us in the crises of life.

Present and future rewards are a vital part of the believer's heritage. The Lord tells us how to live, gives us the necessary power, then rewards us with blessings in this life and crowns in the one to come. You can't beat that!

34

Finally we must mention *eternal life*. This means far more than endless existence. It is a quality of life, nothing less than the life of Christ in the believer. It is a present possession which will continue eternally.

As we said, this is only a partial list of the blessings that are ours in Christ Jesus. The world can offer none of them.

Therefore every child of God should be able to say:

> *O worldly pomp and glory,*
> *Your charms are spread in vain!*
> *I've heard a sweeter story!*
> *I've found a truer gain!*
> *Where Christ a place prepareth,*
> *There is my loved abode;*
> *There shall I gaze on Jesus:*
> *There shall I dwell with God.*
> —H. K. Burlingham, 1865,
> from the German

When Satan tempted the Lord Jesus, he showed Him all the kingdoms of the world and their glory in a moment of time (Lk. 4:5). It didn't take long. It will take all eternity for God to reveal to His people "the exceeding riches of His grace in His kindness toward us in Christ Jesus" (Eph. 2:7).

9

DIFFERENT FACES OF THE WORLD

The world controls every aspect of human behavior except the true Christian church. There is the world of politics, of business, of culture, of the mass media, of education, of entertainment, and even of religion. These may all appear very attractive from the outside, but behind the scenes they are corrupt. Politics is by its very nature corrupt; it is a system of graft, bribery, and compromises. Business is corrupt; it is shot through with unethical practices. Culture is corrupt; it glorifies sex, nudity, and nihilism. The mass media are corrupt; they aggressively report crime, violence, scandal, and perversion while treating decency and nobility with studied contempt. Education is corrupt; it glorifies human wisdom which, after centuries, has proved itself to be bankrupt. The entertainment world is corrupt; in a world of fantasy, it idolizes prostitutes, perverts, and punks. In some senses, the religious world is the worst of all; it leads people down the primrose path to hell with the delusion that they can save themselves by their good works and good character.

In It But Not Of It

I said that the world controls every aspect of human behavior except the true Christian church. Unfortunately it often affects even the church. One keen observer of the current scene said, "I looked for the church and found it in the world. I looked for the world and found it in the church."[15]

Shortly before his death, Francis Schaeffer warned:

> *To accommodate to the world spirit about us in our age is the most gross form of worldliness in the proper definition of the word.* And unhappily today we must say that in general the evangelical establishment has been accommodating to the form of the world spirit as it finds expression in our day . . . in the most basic sense, the evangelical establishment has become deeply worldly.

And Wordsworth wrote:

> *The world is too much with us; late and soon,*
> *Getting and spending, we lay waste our powers.*

Politics. Now let us think of the world of politics. We often hear the well-worn argument, "All that is necessary for evil to triumph is for good men to do nothing." The trouble is that that is worldly opinion, not divine revelation. We are also reminded that Joseph, Moses, and Daniel engaged in politics. Actually Joseph and Daniel were civil servants, not men who ran for office. And Moses was a thorn in the side of the political establishment in Egypt.

What is the scriptural testimony on the subject?

Jesus said, "My kingdom is not of this world. If My kingdom were of this world, My servants, would fight" (Jn. 18:36).

Paul said, "No one engaged in warfare entangles himself with the affairs of this life" (2 Tim. 2:4).

John said, "The whole world lies under the sway of the wicked one" (1 Jn. 5:19).

The example of the Lord Jesus is against political participation. He was in an adversary relationship to the establishment. The apostles did not resort to politics. Their order was to go into all the world and preach the gospel.

The Christian's primary citizenship is heavenly (Phil. 3:20). His obligation to earthly government is to pray, pay, and obey.

God's purpose in this age is not political reform, but to take out of the nations a people for His Name (Acts 15:14). The question is, "Are we going to follow His agenda?"

The basic problem in the world is sin. Only the gospel can deal successfully with that. God's method is spiritual—the new birth.

Politics by its very nature is corrupt. If I participate, I cast a vote of confidence in it. Such confidence is completely unjustified. It has had hundreds of years to prove its effectiveness and what has been the outcome?

The record of Christians in politics has not been good. William Kelly said, "Never have Christians meddled with governing the world except to Christ's dishonor and their own shame. They are now called to suffer with Christ; by and by they shall reign with Him. Even He has not yet taken His great power for reigning."[16]

The time for believers to rule has not come yet. It will come when Christ returns as King of kings and Lord of lords. When the Corinthians acted as if they were already reigning, Paul corrected them. He wished that they were reigning so that he and the other apostles could reign with them. But while the Corinthians were, in a figure, wearing their crowns in box seats in the amphitheater, the apostles were like men in the arena, condemned to death, a spectacle to the world, and treated as the scum of the earth (1 Cor. 4:8-13).

It is a false expectation to think that conditions in the world are going to improve (1 Tim 4:1-3; 2 Tim. 3:1-5). Both the Bible and the daily news refute such a notion.

The Christian finds power in separation from the world (2 Cor. 6:17). We can never move it as long as we are a part of it. Our great resource is prayer. We can do more through prayer than others can do in politics. We can see miraculous transformations of human lives. We can pray men and women into the kingdom of God. We hold the balance of power in the world. Why barter this for a bankrupt system of politics?

Business. It is easy to think that the business world is honest, ethical, and humane, but that is not realistic. The drive for megabucks makes it an arena of cutthroat competition. It's a jungle out there. Ethics are sacrificed to profits and people are sacrificed to the bottom line. The government passes laws to curb abuses, but there are always ways of circumventing the laws. Bookkeeping tricks hide profits from taxation and money passed under the table opens doors for making a fast dollar.

The Christian cannot live in isolation from the business world. The simple activity of living involves him in it. He would have to go out of the world to be completely free from it. However, he can use it without abusing it (1 Cor. 7:31). He can work, buy, and sell without adopting its methods that are shady. He can be salt and light in the office, shop, or factory (Mt. 5:13-14). He can refuse to compromise his testimony by stooping to anything that would dishonor his Lord. Of course, there are some occupations which are out of bounds for a believer; he cannot involve himself in any activity that is illegal or that is physically or morally harmful to others.

Culture. Then there is the world of culture—the world of art and of music. Surely there is nothing objectionable in the humanities. Nothing wrong? The National Endowment for the Arts, subsidized by the federal government, sponsored a painting that portrayed Jesus Christ in a setting so vile, so repulsive, that it cannot be described in decent literature. And the lyrics of much music is suggestive, provocative, and obscene.

But what about art and music that are uplifting? The saint can enjoy the talents that God has given to others, but he is here for bigger business than to be a connoisseur of fine art. As long as souls are perishing for want of the gospel of Jesus, he must concentrate on what is of eternal value. When Paul visited Athens, the center of culture, he was not impressed by the Parthenon or the Temple. He was impelled to tell out the excellencies of the One who had called him out of darkness into marvelous light.

The Media. What about the media? It's the world's propaganda arm. Its job is to "sell" the world. Therefore it reports news about its own personalities and happenings. You couldn't expect any respectful mention of Christ on the first page of the newspaper. Nor should you look for anything that is spiritually edifying in the average TV program. Sometimes Christians are tempted to resent the fact that the press, TV, and radio report violence, glorify sin and shame, and treat decency with studied neglect. They give the headlines to Hollywood prostitutes with hardly a mention of godly men and women of whom the world is not worthy. Well, that's the way it should be. Why should they publicize their rival kingdom?

And anyway it is better that God's people should travel through the world incognito. "The world does not know us, because it did not know Him" (1 Jn. 3:1b). When Christ appears, we will appear with Him in glory (see Col. 3:4). That will be soon enough to hit the headlines. James Denney said it well: "No Christian should be ambitious of anything but to fill as unobtrusively as possible the place in life which God has given him. The less notorious we are, the better for us."[17]

One news station is more accurate than it realizes when it advertises, "Giving you the world every 30 minutes." And so is the TV station with the slogan, "Bringing the world into your home."

Education. What shall we say about education? A certain amount is both desirable and necessary. We want our children and young people to be well educated. But the catchword in that sentence is "well." So the Christian must walk a tight line. He must separate the precious from the vile, must eat the chicken and spit out the bones.

Secular education is chaos today. Those in authority experiment with every harebrained suggestion that comes along and fail to teach the basics. When the public awakens to the system's failure, the educators cry for more money. It isn't more dollars they need; it's more sense.

The world refuses to offer education that is not adulterated. It laces facts with fiction. It parades theories as truth. Refusing to acknowledge the Creator, it attributes design and order to "nature." It boasts of its liberality, but is viciously intolerant of the Bible or anything the Bible teaches. "Every major idea and philosophy shaping our world right now is opposed to New Testament Christianity and intends to wipe it from the face of the earth."[17]

Entertainment. Another face of the world is its entertainment system. This is the world of the movies, TV, radio—you name it. Bunyan called it Vanity Fair. It is the world of smutty innuendos, suggestive body language, and sensuous styles. Not only does it popularize sin, it ridicules chastity and purity. It glorifies sex, violence, and all that cheapens life. In describing current movies, a noted film critic used such expressions as unrelieved ugliness, horror and depravity, and vivid brutality.[18] Its hidden agenda is to amuse people on their way to hell, to keep them from thinking about eternal issues. Entertainers create the impression that pleasure is fulfillment. Then one night at home, they ask, "Is this all there is?" and put a pistol to their head.

Religion. Just as there are only two worlds, so there are only two religions. The world's religion puts self on the throne and teaches salvation by works or character. It has a form of godliness, but denies the power of it.

It has a broad tolerance for every belief except the true gospel and for everyone except a fundamentalist Christian.

It abandons the Bible as the inspired Word of God, leaving itself to the shifting sands of human opinion. There are no absolutes; everything is relative.

It replaces God with humanism, believing that man is the master of his fate and the captain of his soul.

42

It seeks to silence true prophets. The only kind it likes are false ones who follow the party line or true ones who are dead.

It was the religious world that crucified the Lord of glory. To have fellowship with it is to be a traitor to Christ.

The Lord Jesus is outside this monstrous system, and He calls His followers to walk in separation from it. They must go forth to Him, outside the camp, bearing His reproach (Heb. 13:11-14). This includes separation from the ungodly ecumenical mixture of believers and unbelievers so common in Christendom today.

Yes, in all these areas, a disciple must take his place outside the existing order of things. His strength lies in his separation. Archimedes said he could move the world if he could have a fulcrum outside it. So can the believer, but he must be outside it.

10

TWO WISDOMS: VIVID CONTRASTS

Let's think now of the wisdom of the world and contrast it with the wisdom of our King and His kingdom. By his own wisdom, man could never know God. He thinks that the preaching of the gospel is utter nonsense, but God in His wisdom uses it to save those who believe (1 Cor. 1:21). Man would never choose foolish, weak, base, despised, or insignificant things to accomplish his purposes. But God has chosen them, and with them He puts the wise and mighty to shame and reduces to size those whom the world considers great (1 Cor. 1:27-28).

In these and other ways, He makes foolish the wisdom of this world. No wonder Paul said, "The wisdom of this world is foolishness with God. For it is written, 'He catches the wise in their own craftiness" (1 Cor. 3:19). Traill was even stronger: he said, "Wisdom outside of Christ is damning folly."

The world's greatest folly is its rejection of the Word of God. This leaves it without an infallible authority and casts it adrift on a sea of human opinion. Make no mistake about it; man either accepts God's truth or human opinion. And if opinion, then the predicament is "Whose opinion is right?" It is one person's idea against another's. Often the most vocal opinions are the ones that carry, no matter how senseless or deviant they might be.

The Christian has a firm foundation—the Word of God. He has an absolute standard by which to judge words, thoughts, and actions. He tests all opinions by the sacred Scriptures.

Man's opinions may budge, but God's law won't.

With the Bible, there are absolutes. There are things that are right, and things that are wrong. But reject the Bible and everything is relative. Thus, you cannot say that things are wrong in themselves. Drunkenness and drug addiction may be in the genes or may be nothing more than an illness. Homosexuality is an acceptable lifestyle. Fornication is all right as long as it's done in love. Human life is sacred except when it comes to abortion. Discipline of children is taboo. Marriage is nothing more than a legal paper and can be broken for any cause. The door is wide open for radical feminism, psychological seduction, humanism, Eastern mysticism, occultism, and idolatry. It's what people think about these things that matters.

The world exalts man and man's intellect. The believer exalts the Word of God, and knows that the fear of the Lord is the beginning of wisdom (Ps. 111:10).

The world puts a premium on the majority, on big numbers. Voltaire said that God is on the side of the big battalions. God puts a premium on quality. He reduces Gideon's army from 32,000 to 22,000 and then to 300, so that the victory would obviously be the Lord's. Jesus chose only twelve disciples, not 1,200. With God, the majority is not always right; usually it is the despised minority, the faithful remnant. E. Stanley Jones said, "I hate this scramble for numbers that leads to collective egotism."

The world says, "Be true to yourself." The Christian way is to live for others, esteeming them better than self (Phil. 2:3).

The world's conventional wisdom is to save your life. Christ counsels His followers to lose their lives for His sake and the gospel (Mk. 8:35).

For the world, greatness is in being served, being master and lord (Lk. 22:25). The Lord Jesus showed by word and example that greatness is to serve (Lk. 22:26-27). "Self thinks itself great and is served. Love serves and is great."

The man of the world pushes for the top, for fame, and for status. But Christian discipleship is a downward path of self-emptying (Phil. 2:7).

> *Love has a hem to its garment*
> *That touches the very dust.*
> *It can reach the stains of the streets and lanes*
> *And because it can, it must.*

The world measures riches through the abundance of its possessions. The believer measures his through the fewness of his wants. The rich fool accumulates material things. The wise Christian forsakes all for Christ. The worldling lays up treasures on earth, the disciple in heaven.

The wisdom of the world is foolishness with God. The foolishness of God is wiser than men.

However, the Lord Jesus made the startling concession that there is one way in which "the sons of this world are more shrewd in their generation than the sons of light" (Lk. 16:8). Unbelievers make provision for their future; the future, as far as they are concerned is here on earth. Sons of light fail to make provision for their future in heaven; they live for the things of time and sense instead of for eternal realities.

You call THAT Wisdom?

Actually, the wisdom of the world is foolish on the face of it. Let me give you some examples:

Many men of the world are atheists. It is an irrational position. It actually claims for itself omniscience and omnipresence (I know that there is no God anywhere in the universe) and denies the plainest evidence.

Evolution is an essential tenet of the world system. Man knows that if there is a Creator-God, then he is responsible to Him, and such a thought is completely unacceptable. Because he does not want to retain God in his knowledge, he adheres to evolution, saying, in effect, that nothing created something out of nothing; that you can have design without a designer. It is irrational!

The world's psychology attempts to explain human behavior, but is adamant in refusing to acknowledge the existence of original sin. It is impossible to explain why people act as they do unless we see that they are sinners by nature and practice.

Crime is blamed on parents or on the environment. This, of course, is an attempt to eliminate human responsibility. It won't work. A person is influenced not only by heredity and environment, but even more by his own will.

God warns people against committing various sins, and outlines the punishment that follows disobedience. Man plunges ahead into sin, suffers the consequences, then turns around and blames God. It is just as the Bible says, "When a man's folly brings his way to ruin, his heart rages against the Lord" (Prov. 19:3 RSV). Is that a demonstration of wisdom— or even fairness?

The following two stickers appeared on the same bumper: Save the whales. Abortion: A Woman's Right.

Toy guns are outlawed in San Francisco, but not real ones.

TV shows teach people how to pull off successful crimes, then society punishes them when they do it.

A murderer was allowed to plead diminished capacity because he ate too many Twinkies (junk food). He received a reduced sentence.

The U.S. government subsidizes the raising of tobacco, then requires cigarette makers to warn users that cigarettes may be harmful to their health.

Alcoholism is now recognized by the world as a disease. It is the only disease that is contracted by an act of the will, sold in bottles, given as a gift, taxed by governments, is habit forming, and keeps the patient out of heaven.

Thousands of dollars are spent to save the northern owl

and the snail darter from extinction while millions of unborn children are murdered in aborturaries.

Christmas is celebrated nationally, but Christmas carols are banned in many public schools.

· Discipline of children is frowned on, then the parents wonder why they go wild. For many years Dr. Benjamin Spock's book, *Baby and Child Care,* was treated as a bible by a generation of parents. Years later, he admitted that he and other "experts" were to blame for today's bratty children. He said, "Inability to be firm is, to my mind, the commonest problem of parents in America today. Parental submissiveness only encourages children to be more pesky and demanding. It makes unpleasantness unavoidable."[19] Parents could have saved themselves a lot of heartache if they had followed the book of Proverbs instead of Spock.

Teachers are not allowed to give an aspirin to a pupil without parental consent, or take children on a field trip, but often teenage girls can get an abortion legally without their parents' knowledge.

Whenever a catastrophic accident occurs, the government appoints a commission to investigate the cause. This is often an attempt to deflect attention from a failure to enforce safety regulations. Money and lives might have been saved by taking preventive action.

The United States spent half a million dollars to study the effect of cigarette smoking on dogs, and 19 million to see if belching by cows and other livestock harms the ozone.

11
MODUS OPERANDI

Let us think now of the methods generally employed by the world system. It is customary to help those who help you. To persecute non-conformists. To fight back, giving tit for tat. To use violence if necessary. To do the least amount possible for the greatest reward. To show favoritism. To distribute according to greed (Mt. 20:1-16). To outdo others in a spirit of competition (Jas. 3:14-16). To resort to graft, bribery, corruption.

Not so in Christ's kingdom. There you help those who cannot repay (Lk. 14:12-14). While suffering for righteousness' sake (1 Pet. 2:20), you show love to all (Rom. 13:8). You repay evil with good (Rom. 12:20; 1 Thess. 5:15). You practice non-resistance, turning the other cheek (Lk. 6:27-29). You go the second mile (Mt. 5:41). You show kindness to all, do good to all men (Gal. 6:10). You distribute according to need, not greed (Mt. 20:1-16). You prefer cooperation over competition (1 Cor. 12:25). And you are strictly honest, refusing to indulge in any shady practice (Rom. 14:17).

12

THE WEAPONS OF OUR WARFARE

The world uses carnal weapons. Here we do not confine ourselves to guns, tanks, warships, and bombers. Money is most often used as a carnal weapon; the world believes that money answers everything, and that every man has his price. Propaganda can be used as a carnal weapon. Flattery is a common tool. And the psychological manipulation of people.

Let me mention five smart bombs in the Christian armory, all life-giving, not death dealing

There is love (Lk. 6:27-35). This is not to be confused with natural affection. Everyone has that; there is nothing distinctive about it. Christian love is supernatural, one that can be shown only by the power of the Holy Spirit. It goes out to the unlovely and unlovable. It lends and asks nothing in return. It turns the other cheek and goes the second mile. It lavishes itself on enemies. It treats others as the giver would want to be treated. People of the world can't stand before a barrage like that.

Prayer is a weapon (Eph. 6:18). It can move God to do things He would not otherwise have done (Jas. 4:2). It can reach out and move men through God. It can change the destiny of nations. Man never comes closer to omnipotence than when he prays in the Name of the Lord Jesus. The world might legislate against gospel preaching, but there is no way by which they can stop prayer. Said Ronald Dunn, "Intercession is the secret weapon of the secret kingdom. The early Christians knew this and, refusing to bow to Caesar, they prayed for him. It is remarkable that both Paul and Peter admonished their readers to pray for and honor the very person who was waging bloody persecution against them—the king (1 Tim. 2:1,2; 1 Pet. 2:17)."[20]

The Bible is a weapon. Like no other book, this sword of the Spirit is living, powerful, and sharper than any steel sword (Heb. 4:12). It can illuminate the darkest heart. It can plunge the most ungodly into deep conviction of sin. It can bring the new birth to the lost, helpless, and hopeless. It can give beauty for ashes, the oil of joy for mourning, and the garment of praise for the spirit of heaviness (Isa. 61:3).

Another weapon is a Christlike life. Such a life is a fact that men can't argue against (Acts 4:14). It is one thing to read the truth in a book or tract, but it is quite another thing to see the truth made flesh in a human life. People of the world may not like it (it is so convicting), but they'll never forget it.

Faith is a weapon that overcomes the world (1 Jn. 5:4). It makes the unseen visible and the future present. It feeds on problems and is not deterred by impossibilities. It wins battles, overthrows kingdoms, preserves believers from lions and fire. It can move mountains, dry up a sea, and give life to the dead.

All the Christian's weapons are spiritual, not carnal; mighty, not powerless. The world's weapons are toy guns by comparison.

13

THE WORLD'S EMPTY HONORS

The world motivates people with flashy uniforms and with honors such as plaques, diplomas, ribbons, medals, titles, trophies, loving cups. Napoleon once held up a piece of ribbon and said, "With these I could build a kingdom."

For money a man will work tirelessly, travel incessantly, endanger his health, neglect his family, give the best years of his life to a faceless corporation, only to be dismissed when he is no longer needed or when his powers begin to fail.

He will push his body to the limit in order to achieve athletic fame. For a prestigious title, he will count no sacrifice too great. What will he not do to see his name in a professional journal or the local newspaper?

All the world's honors are empty. They are quickly forgotten and void of any lasting value.

Spurgeon said that "the world pays scantily indeed. What will it do for those it loves the best? When it has done all it can, the last resource of the world is to give a man a title (and what is that?). And then to give him a tall pillar and set him up there to bear all weathers, to be pitilessly exposed to every storm; and there he stands for fools to gaze at, one of the world's great ones paid in stone. It is that which the world has paid out of its heart, for that is what the world's heart is made of." [21]

14
HONORS THAT MATTER

"The world pays niggardly and scantily, but did you ever hear a Christian who complained thus of his Master? 'No,' he will say, 'when I serve Christ, I feel that my work is my wages; that labor for Christ is its own reward. He gives me joy on earth, with a fullness of bliss hereafter.' Oh, Christ is a good paymaster! . . . He that serves Christ may get but little gold and silver such as this world calls precious, but he gets a gold and a silver that shall ne'er be melted in the last refining fire, that shall glitter among the precious things of immortality throughout eternity. The world pays niggardly and scantily but not so Christ." [22]

The Christian sees through the worthlessness of earth's honors. "If we are His, we have nothing to do with anything, even the prettiest shred of this world's glory. Be assured, it is only a patch of dishonor for the child of God now. It matters not what the world's prize may be. Why should we want it? Are not all things ours? Shall we not judge the world—aye, even angels? I do not dwell on the fact that these present objects so often bear the very stamp of their own insignificance and worthlessness upon them, that their wise men confess that the good is in the chase, not in the game. Who does not know that even a 'ribbon' is enough reward for someone's lifelong exertions! These otherwise are sensible men. What would not the richest and noblest do or endure for a garter (emblem of a British Order).[23]

Amy Carmichael, intrepid missionary to India, "coveted

no place on earth but the dust at the foot of the Cross." In January, 1919, she, along with others, was notified that she was to be honored by the king of England. She wrote a courteous refusal, saying, "It troubles me to have an experience so different from His who was despised and rejected, not kindly honored."[24] Under extreme persuasion, she finally agreed to accept it, but did not go to Madras for the ceremony.

Baron von Welz, a wealthy estate owner in Holland, was overcome with a love for the Lord Jesus and a desire to carry the gospel to the perishing. He ceased to love his title and treasures, and set out as a missionary to Dutch Guinea. Before leaving, he said:

> What to me is the title "well-born," when I am born again in Christ? What to me is the title "lord," when I desire to be a servant of His? What is it to me to be called "your grace," when, moment by moment, I have need of God's grace, help, and succor? Away with all these vanities, and everything beside I will lay at the feet of Jesus, my dearest Lord, that I may have no hindrance in serving Him aright. [25]

William Kelly is another case in point. When his nephew went to the university, his professors were impressed by his knowledge of Greek. When asked, the nephew explained that he had been tutored by his uncle, William Kelly. Later, when there was a vacancy in the Greek faculty, a delegation visited Kelly and invited him to take the post. They couldn't understand his refusal. Finally one said in exasperation, "What's the matter, Mr. Kelly, don't you want to make a name for yourself in the world?" He replied simply, "Which world, gentlemen?"

Said Dave Hunt, "It would be a denial of their Lord for Christians to bask in the popularity and honors that this present world may bestow upon them. That is not to say that a Christian should never be successful in business, science, the academic world, sports, etc. Indeed, Christians should be the very best they can possibly be at whatever they do. But their skill, talent, and diligent efforts are expended for God's glory, not for their own. This world has no attraction for believers; they neither love it nor its plaudits. They are not swayed from the course they must run (1 Cor. 9:24-27; 2 Tim. 4:7-8) either by the world's criticism or its compliments. They know that ultimately nothing matters except God's opinion of them."[26]

In a very real sense, the service of Christ is its own reward. I am reminded of a woman who pointed to her dog and said, "This dog wants only two things. He wants to know what I want him to do, and he wants to do it." A trainer of sheep dogs said, "You don't have to reward those dogs. It is enough for them to be out on the hillsides, obeying the shepherd's whistles." But there are other rewards for the believer. There are the crowns at the end of the journey—the crown of glory, of righteousness, of life. And best of all, the Saviour's "Well done, good and faithful servant. . . . Enter into the joy of your Lord" (Mt. 25:23).

Michael Griffith asks, "What will we have to show for our life? Will it be measured by life's little rewards and successes, some certificates of education, some silver cups indicative of athletic prowess, a few medals, some newspaper cuttings, promotion within our profession, some status in the local community, a presentation clock on retirement, an obituary notice, and a well-attended funeral? Is that all that our life will have meant?"[27]

John Sung, the Chinese evangelist, was returning home after earning a doctorate in the United States. As the vessel neared the end of the voyage, he went down to his cabin, gathered up his diplomas, his medals, and his fraternity keys, and threw them overboard. . . . Some days later, he had a dream in which he saw himself in a coffin, dressed in academic cap and gown, and holding a diploma. He heard a voice say, "John Sung is dead—dead to the world." When the corpse began to show signs of coming back to life, angels above started to weep. John said, "Don't weep, angels. I will remain dead to the world." Through the rest of his life, he carried out this noble resolve.[28]

"These are the pilgrims. . . . For them the royalties and glories; the honors and rewards; the delights and indulgences of men—have no attraction. They are children of a sublimer realm, members of a greater commonwealth, burgesses of a nobler city than any upon which the sun has ever looked. Foreigners may mulct [swindle] an Englishman of all his spending money; but he can well afford to lose it, if all his capital is safely invested at home, in the Bank of England. How can a dukedom in some petty principality present attractions to the scion of an empire, who is passing hastily through this tiny territory, as fast as steam and wealth can carry him, to assume the supreme authority of a mighty monarchy? The pilgrim has no other desire than to pass quickly over the appointed route to his home—a track well trodden through all ages—fulfilling the duties, meeting the claims, and discharging faithfully the responsibilities devolving upon him, but ever remembering that here he has no continuing city, and seeks one which is to come."[29]

To be a child of God is an infinitely greater honor than anything the world can bestow.

15

THE MAN OF THE WORLD

The ideal citizen of the world is a person of money, power, and a scintillating personality. Characteristically he is proud and arrogant. He is no stranger to envy and strife. In his determination to enrich himself, he becomes intolerant of every rival or competitor. When it comes to making money, integrity is thrown to the wind; he is willing to make compromises and resort to unethical practices. He lives to satisfy his natural appetites; in that area, parties and other get-togethers are duds unless enlivened with liquor. Under his immaculate suit may lurk a life of impurity. He has a wife at home and a mistress abroad. His thought life is polluted and his morals debased. Conversation is interspersed with profanity and street language. Other people are of value only as he can "use" them. As for temper, his fuse is short. To confess wrong is weakness to him, and to forgive others is foreign. All told, he fails to rise above flesh and blood.

The man of the world walks by sight, not by faith. To him, seeing is believing. He judges by outward appearances. To him beauty is "the golden coin of human worth."

Dr. James Dobson writes that "Physical beauty is the most highly valued personal attribute in our culture. . . . Thus a beautiful child is more favored by adults than a plain one. Teachers tend to give better grades to attractive children. Pretty children get less discipline than others. Homely children are more subject to blame for misdemeanors. And this form of discrimination continues through adolescence and into adult life."[30]

J. B. Phillips gives the following version of the Beatitudes, as practiced by the men of the world:

Happy are the pushers: for they get on in the world.

Happy are the hard-boiled: for they never let life hurt them.

Happy are they who complain: for they get their own way in the end.

Happy are the blasé: for they never worry over their sins.

Happy are the slave-drivers: for they get results.

Happy are the knowledgeable men of the world: for they know their way around.

Happy are the trouble-makers: for people have to take notice of them.[31]

16

THE MAN OF GOD

Jesus described the ideal citizen of His kingdom in the Beatitudes. He is poor in spirit, a mourner, a hungerer for justice, merciful, pure in heart, a peacemaker, and patient under persecution (Mt. 5:3-12). In His public ministry, the Lord Jesus was always speaking of His followers as the last, the lowest, the least, the poor, the disinherited (see Jas. 2:5). The man of God is other-worldly, an enigma to his unsaved friends. In words and deeds, he makes people think of Christ. He is gentle, mild-mannered, and tenderhearted. Never vindictive, he is ready to forgive those who have wronged him. His life is free from partiality, hypocrisy, dishonesty, and immorality. He can talk without swearing, have a good time without alcohol. For him to live is Christ, and to die is gain.

The child of God walks by faith, not by sight (2 Cor. 5:7). It is because he looks through the eyes of faith that a prayer meeting is more desirable than a baseball game; that the work of a church elder is more important than the presidency of the United States; that an obscure missionary counts for more than the most successful businessman; that Bible study is more exhilarating than watching a television documentary; that the church is more important to God than the greatest empire. When a person walks by faith, he will do for Christ what he would never do for dollars. To him, believing is seeing. He judges according to righteous judgment, not according to looks.

"The Christian media fawns over a sports hero, an attractive actress, a wealthy businessman, or a highly-placed politician who has supposedly become a Christian. These too-often immature, worldly new believers are paraded and lauded on Christian TV—and held up to the church as heroes of the faith, role models for youth—and Christians turn out by the thousands to 'ooh' and 'aah' at their 'testimonies.' Yet the humble, godly missionary, mature in the faith, who has remained true to Christ through decades of privation, temptation, hardship, and danger, and has won souls in difficult fields of labor, can scarcely draw an audience. Obviously the average Christian admires worldly success far more than godliness. Something is badly askew."[32]

17
WHAT ABOUT SOCIAL CONCERNS?

In recent years, some prominent Christian leaders have outspokenly criticized evangelicals for not being more involved in social programs for world betterment. The impression they leave is that believers have been religious obscurantists, contenting themselves with preaching the gospel while the world is going to pot. Christians should be more concerned with bodies than souls. How can they expect hungry, oppressed people to be interested in a message that offers pie in the sky but none right now? And so the indictment reads.

What is the answer to this type of charge?

No one denies for one moment that Christians should seek to alleviate human need and suffering. The Lord Jesus is our example. He went around doing good, healing all who were oppressed by the devil, restoring the sick, giving sight to the blind, and feeding the multitude. In the story of the good Samaritan, He left no doubt as to our obligation to our neighbor, which means anyone in need. Actually Christians have always been in the forefront of charitable programs, such as hospitals, orphanages, city missions, and educational institutions. Having said that, we must never forget that the believer's first priority is the gospel (Mt. 28:19-20). God's present purpose is not the improvement of the world. Rather it is to call out of the nations a people for His Name (Acts 15:14). If we are to be working with the Lord, this must be our goal also.

The gospel is the only solution to man's problems. His

spiritual needs are greater than his physical or social needs. The root of his trouble is sin, and only the gospel deals with that. Most human remedies are nothing better than band-aids. As Jeremiah said, "They have healed the hurt of the daughter of my people slightly" (Jer. 8:11).

It is true that the gospel has social implications. In the context of our daily lives, we are to do good to all men—to feed the hungry, to clothe the naked, to show mercy to the sick, to visit those in prison. But historically, Christian churches and organizations that move into the field of humanitarian programs end up de-emphasizing the gospel. Social involvement must never crowd out our number one priority.

We must constantly remind ourselves that world improvement is not our calling. We are not appointed to make the world a better place in which to live. The bottom line is regeneration, not reformation. The world system is under God's curse, so why work against God?

Furthermore, we have no biblical mandate for joining with unbelievers in trying to set the world straight. The testimony of Scripture is to the contrary. Listen! "Should you help the wicked and love those who hate the Lord?" (2 Chron. 19:2b). "Can two walk together unless they are agreed?" (Amos 3:3). "Do not be unequally yoked together with unbelievers. For what fellowship has righteousness with lawlessness? And what communion has light with darkness? And what accord has Christ with Belial? Or what part has a believer with an unbeliever?" (2 Cor. 6:14).

Believers who contemplate involving themselves in the reformation of abuses should take a biblical perspective. Here are some examples:

Antiwar crusades. Demonstrations for peace are an exercise in futility. Two thousand years ago, the world rejected the Prince of Peace and nailed Him to a felon's cross. Since then, this planet has never been wholly free from war. And there will never be peace until the Lord Jesus returns and sets up

His kingdom. Man does not know how to make peace. Conflict is endemic to fallen human nature. Peace is desirable, but it is unattainable under present conditions. All the peace rallies, the bumper stickers, the billboards will never change that fact. They are a waste of time and money.

Worldwide food programs. Who would dare to discourage rushing aid to victims of famine or catastrophe? Human decency and compassion demand it. But the disturbing truth is that while people in a given area may suffer hunger, there is no shortage of food in the world. The problem is with false religion and human greed. One false religion, for instance, forbids eating meat. People die while "sacred cows" roam the countryside, living off handouts from the impoverished. Foreign governments send grain, but the rats eat more of it than humans do, because the people won't kill rats. Then there is the problem of distribution. Human greed diverts food from those who need it. It withholds supplies from despised ethnic minorities and from those who are on the wrong side of the political or religious fence. It does not want food distributed freely because that would be bad for business. Only the gospel attacks false religion and human greed. That is why Christ is the answer to the world's need.

As we said, believers have always been in the forefront of humanitarian efforts. They respond to genuine cases of need. They are quick to send relief in times of famine; it is the Christian thing to do. The problem comes when this becomes the major activity and crowds out the gospel. In normal times, there are plenty of people to handle relief. Jesus said, "Let the dead bury their own dead, but you go and preach the kingdom of God" (Lk. 9:60).

Anti-abortion crusades. There is no question that abortion is murder. There is no question that militant pro-lifers are sincere and often willing to endure imprisonment for the cause. But here is another case where the good is the enemy of the best. Picket lines do not permanently deter a woman who is set on getting rid of her unborn. Demonstrations against abortion do not change human nature. Would it not be better to spend the time preaching the gospel and witnessing for Christ? It's a question of priorities.

Military service. With regard to military service, there are very strong arguments pro and con. Killing others is contrary to the teaching and spirit of Christ. He said, "My kingdom is not of this world. If my kingdom were of this world, My servants would fight . . . but now My kingdom is not from here" (Jn. 18:36). He also said, "All who take the sword will perish by the sword" (Mt. 26:52). On the other hand, is it really God's will that the armed forces be completely without salt and light, without any Christian witness? Are those who bear arms any more guilty than those who make uniforms, weapons, or anything else that in any way contributes to the war effort? And what about police officers who bear arms and who are acknowledged as God's ministers (Rom. 13:4). If we would defend our wife and children from an intruder, why not do so on a national level? As we said, there are arguments on both sides. In such a situation, what is a Christian to do? My answer is that if he is faced with the question of service in the armed forces, he should go before the Lord and ask for a clear indication of God's will for him in this particular situation. It may be that the Lord will lead him to be a conscientious objector, or to participate as a non-combatant, or to enlist with the goal, not of killing, but serving as a missionary to those who are facing death. It cannot be denied that the military is one of the greatest mission fields in the world. If God leads someone into the armed forces, those who sit comfortably at home should not look down their pacifistic noses in judgment on him. Neither should anyone sit in judgment on those who are called to be conscientious objectors or non-combatants.

Civil Disobedience. A Christian is never justified in engaging in civil disobedience. His first obligation is to obey human government. But of course there is a limit. If the government requires him to disobey the Lord, then he must refuse. Even then, however, he does not rebel against authority. Instead, he meekly bears the punishment for such refusal.

18
CONCLUSION

Two kingdoms, but worlds apart! They could not be more opposite. One is an evil empire, the other a realm of holiness. One is shallow, sham, and show. The other is a realm of realism.

Christ died to deliver us from this present evil world (Gal. 1:4). "So perilous is this age in its temptations, and so awful in its coming judgments, that one great object of our Lord's whole mission was to deliver us from it; and those who live in it, but are not of it, are like travelers on a mountaintop, or Moses upon Pisgah, they see things in their relations; they compare the desert with the land of promise, the present evil age with the coming age of glory, and so actually foretaste the age to come, and get a growing distaste of the age that now is."[33]

We are crucified to the world and the world to us (Gal. 6:14). The cross is all our glory. It is sheer folly for a Christian to give the best years of his life to worldly pursuits, then give the burned-out end of a wasted career to the Lord. Thomas H. Gill said it well:

> *I would not give the world my heart,*
> *And then profess Thy love;*
> *I would not feel my strength depart,*
> *And then Thy service prove.*
>
> *I would not with swift winged zeal*
> *On the world's errands go;*

*And labor up the heavenly hill
With weary feet and slow.*

*O choose me in my golden time,
In my dear joys have part!
For Thee the glory of my prime,
The fullness of my heart.*

We are not to be conformed to the world. When marines are being trained, the goal is to destroy their civilian personality with its thought patterns and behavior, and to rebuild them in the marine mold. Likewise, God wants us to throw off our worldly thought patterns and lifestyle and remake us in the image of the Lord Jesus.

The world passes away and the lusts of it. Living for this transient shadow is like rearranging the deck chairs on the Titanic, or straightening the pictures in a burning building. Donald Grey Barnhouse said, "We are not to be interested in the world, for it is a condemned civilization, doomed to be destroyed by the Lord it crucified. The principles, ideals, and methods of our life cannot be mixed with those of the world without being adulterated or contaminated."[34]

A. T. Pierson added:

If you read Revelation 17 and 18, you will find all the things we are boasting about—our commercial supremacy, our martial prowess, our luxury, our extravagance, our inventions, our arts mechanical, and our arts fine—are all presented there in Babylon, which is acknowledged to be 'the great,' even by the angel himself. But its greatness is not of God; and it is going to perish, not by external assault, but by its own rottenness, falling to pieces at last like a broken egg-shell. You had better come out of it, if you do not want to be involved in its plagues.[35]

Luther had the right perspective when he said, "The em-

pire of the whole world is but a crust to be thrown to a dog."
So let the determination of our heart be:

> *Take the world but give me Jesus,*
> *All its joys are but a name;*
> *But His love abideth ever.,*
> *Through eternal years the same.*
> —Fanny Crosby

In Hoc Signo

> *The kingdoms of the earth go by*
> *In purple and in gold;*
> *They rise, they triumph, and they die,*
> *And all their tale is told.*
>
> *One kingdom only is divine,*
> *One Banner triumphs still:*
> *Its King a servant, and its sign*
> *A gibbet on a hill.*
> —Godfrey Fox Bradby

ENDNOTES

1. *The Ministry of Keswick, First Series,* Grand Rapids: Zondervan Publishing House, 1963, p. 110.

2. *The Boston Herald,* November 15, 1990.

3. Dr. J. H. Jowett, further documentation unavailable.

4. F. B. Meyer, *The Christ Life for Your Life,* Chicago: Moody Press, n.d., p. 78.

5. *The Best that I Can Be,* Singapore: OMF Books, 1965, pp. 72, 73.

6. *Lord of What's Left,* Grand Rapids: Baker Book House, 1982, p. 83.

7. *The Keswick Week,* 1983, p. 154.

8. E. Stanley Jones, *Growing Spiritually,* New York: Abingdon Press, 1953, p. 18.

9. *Don't Just Stand There . . . Pray Something,* Amersham-on-the-Hill, England: Scripture Press, 1992, p. 57.

10. *Christianity Today,* January 13, 1989, p. 42.

11. *Today's Choices for Tomorrow's Mission,* Grand Rapids: Academie Books, 1988, p. 199.

12. Ronald Dunn, op. cit, pp. 212-213.

13. Dostoyevsky wrote his niece that he tried to describe a person of moral perfection, but he had to admit that his hero was flawed in many respects. No one can write the story of a perfect person apart from divine inspiration. As Renan said, "It would take a Christ to invent a Christ."

14. *Kingdoms in Conflict,* Grand Rapids: William Morrow/Zondervan Publishing House, 1987, p. 274.

15. *The Great Evangelical Disaster,* Westchester, IL.: Crossway Books, 1984, p. 142.

16. *The Epistles to the Thessalonians,* New York: George Doran Co., n.d., p. 161.

17. Ronald Dunn, op. cit., p. 212.

18. Michael Medved, *The Battle Against Beauty and Truth,* Readers Digest, June 1991, p. 149.

19. *Tampa Tribune,* Fl., January 22, 1974.

20. Op. cit., p. 64.

21. *Words of Wisdom for Daily Life,* Pasadena, TX: Pilgrim publications, nd, p. 104.

22. Ibid.

23. William Kelly, further documentation unavailable.

24. Elisabeth Elliot, *The Person Who Influenced Me Most,* Christianity Today, October 7, 1983, p. 30

25. Quoted in *Uplook* Magazine, February-March 1993, p. 18.

26. C.I.B. Bulletin, Bend, Oregon, May, 1991, p. 1.

27. Further documentation unavailable.

28. Leslie T. Lyall, *John Sung,* Chicago: Moody Press, 1954, pp. 40, 41, 47, 48.

29. F. B. Meyer, *Abraham, Friend of God,* London: Lakeland, 1974, p. 26.

30. *Hide or Seek,* Old Tappan, NJ: Fleming H. Revell Company, 1974.

31. *Your God Is Too Small,* New York: The Macmillan Company, 1958, p. 101.

32. C.I.B. Bulletin, Bend, Oregon, May, 1991, p. 1.

33. Arthur T. Pierson, *Knowing the Scriptures,* NY: Gospel Publishing House, 1910, p. 87.

34. *Genesis,* Grand Rapids: Zondervan Publishing House, 1973, p. 142.

35. *Christ Our Wisdom from God,* The Ministry of Keswick, First Series, Grand Rapids: Zondervan Publishing House, 1963, p. 110.